DOG GROOMING SCISSORS

Sian Somers

UK Book Publishing.com

DOG GROOMING SCISSORS

Editing, design, typesetting and publishing by UK Book Publishing

www.ukbookpublishing.com

ISBN: 978-1-916572-67-6

UK Book Publishing.com

Dedicated to my mum,
thank you so much for all your support and love

Contents

Introduction 1

Chapter 1: What are scissors? 2

Chapter 2: What are Dog Grooming scissors made from? 7

Chapter 3: Types of Grooming scissors and their uses 12

Chapter 4: Right and Left-Handed Scissors 32

Chapter 5: Different Types of Cutting Edges on a Blade 35

Chapter 6: Different Types of Blade Tips 38

Chapter 7: Different Types of Handles 42

Chapter 8: What are Finger Hole and Finger Rests? 46

Chapter 9: What are Bumpers or Stoppers on a
grooming scissor? 49

Chapter 10: How are Grooming Scissors Measured? 53

Chapter 11: How to Hold Grooming Scissors 55

Chapter 12: Scissor Safety 63

Chapter 13: Scissor Tension 65

Chapter 14: A Scissor's Balance 75

Chapter 15: Scissor care and Maintenance 78

Chapter 16: Sharpening Your Grooming Scissors 84

Chapter 17: Potential Problems with Grooming Scissors
and How to fix them 88

Introduction

Becoming a dog groomer is such an exciting experience and a rewarding career, so a massive congratulations on taking the steps into this incredible world.

Scissors are one of the tools of the trade a dog groomer must have. However, the subject of scissors, from what are they, to the types of scissors, to how to hold them and how to look after them, are areas which are seldom taught thoroughly during the current available dog grooming courses in the UK.

This book has been created as a helpful guide to everything a dog groomer or pet owner needs to know about their grooming scissors.

It is a very useful read for all dog groomers, especially those who are learning how to become dog groomers and dog groomers and pet owners who have minimal experience working with and taking care of grooming scissors.

Chapter 1

~~~~

WHAT ARE SCISSORS?

Scissors are hand-operated instruments used to cut cloth, paper, hair, and many other materials. Scissors consist of two blades laid on top of one another and fastened in the middle to allow the blades to be opened and closed by the thumb and fingers inserted through the finer holes at the end of the handle.

There are many types of scissors available nowadays. Dog grooming scissors are designed for all dog breeds and their different coat types.

Who invented scissors?

According to Wikipedia, the earliest known scissors appeared in Mesopotamia between 3000 to 4000 years ago. These scissors were a 'spring scissor' type comprising two bronze blades connected at the handles by a thin, flexible strip of curved bronze, and this served to hold the blades in alignment, to allow them to be squeezed together and cut, and then to pull them apart when released.

The 'spring scissors' were invented by the Romans around 100 AD, but the new 'pivoted scissors' were not introduced across Europe until the 16th Century. The fundamental idea of the pivotal scissor has remained in modern scissor designs.

Scissor Anatomy

Scissors have different components which work in sync to create these incredible cutting tools.

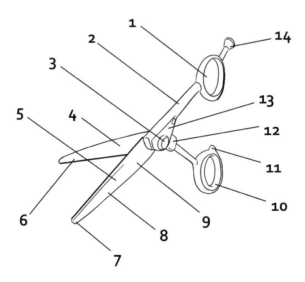

1. Finger hole – This is the place where the fingers are placed. Scissors have a 'finger hole' and a 'thumb hole'.

2. Shaft or Handle – This area attaches the finger holes and pivot together. These can be straight or offset.
3. Pivot or Tension Screw – This holds the blades together and plays a vital role in the blades' cutting action.
4. Inner Blade – This is the side of the blades which physically touch as the blades close and open.
5. Blade Edge – This is the sharp part of the blade.
6. Ride Line – This is the smooth shiny line expanding across the edge of the inner blade.
7. Point or Tip – This is the area where both blades meet when the blades are closed.
8. Spine – This is the thickest part of the blade and the edge is rounded off and not sharp.
9. Outer Blade – This is the side of the blade that shapes the scissors' edge.
10. The Insert Rings or Finger rings – A rubber or plastic ring which fits inside the finger and thumb hole to make the holes smaller to custom fit a hand.
11. Stopper – Rubber or plastic screw in insert that allows the scissor to close at the tip in the correct position and prevents the blades from crossing over.
12. Finger Rest or Tang – This is the area where the fingers rest and provides comfort for reversible scissors. These rests can be fixed or removable.

Is there a difference between hairdressing scissors and dog grooming scissors?

Quite simply, yes.

Grooming scissors are made for dog hair and are different from human hair scissors. Whilst both types of scissors are fundamentally the same, i.e. they both cut hair, the scissors themselves must be different because of the kind of hair they are being used on. Human hair and dog hair, however, differ molecularly.

What is the difference?

Dog fur and human hair are made up of the same exact protein, keratin, which makes them scientifically identical. Keratin is the protein found in both human and dog hair, skin, and nails. Though hair and fur are chemically the same, there are other differentiating factors which means that the scissors used to cut the hair and fur are different.

Humans grow singular hair which grows continuously. One major difference between dog fur and human hair is their molecular composition. While they both consist of the protein keratin, the structure and arrangement of molecules in dog fur and human hair differ, leading to variations in texture and density.

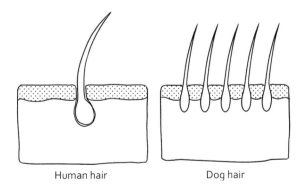

Human hair   Dog hair

As such, the blades and style of scissors for human hair and a dog's coat are designed differently to ensure they cut the hair accordingly. The cutting edges of a dog grooming scissor are designed to be extremely sharp to allow the blades to cut through much coarser hair. Human hair scissors and even paper scissors, would blunt very quickly if they were to be used on a dog's coat. This is because the cutting edges of these types of scissors are designed to be working on softer or finer materials. These scissors are therefore less sharp compared to dog grooming scissors.

When choosing scissors, it is important for the dog groomer to consider the specific coat type they will be working with. Scissors designed for human hair are not suitable for cutting a dog's coat, as they are not sharp enough to cut through the coarser hair.

It is also true that using the wrong type of scissors for the different dog grooming tasks, can cause the blades to blunt prematurely and create undesired finishes, especially on the new mixed poodle coats, terriers and mixed-texture, thick or double coats.

In summary, due to the difference in hair structure of humans and dogs, the techniques and scissors used to cut the hair types must be different. Using the correct dog grooming scissor for the right coat type is vital for a dog groomer.

Chapter 2

~~~

WHAT ARE DOG GROOMING SCISSORS MADE FROM?

Whilst many may believe that scissors are 'just made from steel', the types of steel used make the difference between an unreliable scissor and a very high-end grooming scissor.

Understanding Scissor Steel & The Different Quality types.

It can be challenging to figure out which pair of scissors to buy, with so many brands and models available and with various names and steel types.

Scissor steel quality is determined by the Rockwell Hardness Rating (HRC/HR). In short, this scale measures a scissor's strength and overall hardness. The higher the HRC, the harder the steel, the sharper the cutting edge, the more resistant to corrosion and rust, and the more expensive it is.

So, what is the best steel for Grooming Scissors?

All types of scissors are made from stainless steel, but the best stainless steel comes from Japan. The most popular Japanese stainless steels for scissors are 440c, VG10(VG-10), VG1 (VG-1) and cobalt ATS314 (ATS-314).

These steels create scissors that give shaper edges, require less frequent sharpening, and have a lightweight feel, creating perfect ergonomics.

Scissors made from Japanese Stainless-Steel tend to use sharp convex-edged blades, and the hardened premium steel ensures that the cutting edge remains sharper for longer.

Where does the better-quality stainless steel come from?

1. Japanese Steel: Highest Quality in the world
2. German Steel: Best Quality Steel from Europe
3. Korean Steel: Second Best Steel from Asia
4. Taiwanese Steel: High-Quality Steel
5. Chinese Steel: Great Quality Steel

The lower-quality and less expensive steel is made in India, Pakistan and Vietnam. Due to the quality of the steel itself, the metal tends to be softer. As a result, the cutting edge will blunt quicker and, therefore, can only be sharpened once or twice before the scissors become unusable.

Why is 440C Japanese Stainless Steel the perfect steel for everyday grooming scissors?

Most dog grooming scissors are forged from 440c Japanese stainless steel, as this steel works incredibly well with the structure and coarseness of a dog's coat; the hardness of the steel allows the cutting edge of the blades to remain sharp for a more extended period compared to other metals. This benefit enables a dog groomer to use their scissors for longer between sharpening.

In addition, as the steel is hard, a dog groomer may use the scissors for extended periods, especially throughout an intricate trim or when removing mats. It is the perfect all-rounder in the world of stainless steel.

440c Japanese Stainless Steel is also wonderfully light, so for the dog groomer, this benefit is kinder to their fingers, hands, wrists, and shoulders, and can help prevent future aches and pains associated with dog grooming.

Durable and Rust Free

The science behind this is that stainless steel is an alloy made from steel and chromium. This chemical combination creates a strong alloy that will maintain its sharpness over an extended period. Stainless steel is very tough and, as a result, will drastically increase the blade's durability and lifespan. If the scissor is well maintained, Japanese stainless steel is expected to last between five and ten years. Furthermore, due to the chemical combination of steels such as 440c, rust is extremely unlikely to occur because the alloy is highly resistant to erosion.

Reliable and Easy Maintenance

The fact that stainless steel does not rust easily is a fantastic bonus to a dog groomer. Scissor maintenance is a vital part of owning grooming scissors, but working in a moist environment, as many dog grooming salons are, can mean that the scissors are damp, covered in wet hair, sweat and oils from the dog's coat/skin as well as the groomer's skin, for long periods during the working day. In addition, over time, rust can develop on all metals and alloys, so using a material that reduces the risk of rust is crucial to a scissor's design.

Ergonomically designed Dog Grooming Scissors.

Whilst choosing a new pair scissors, the scissor's sharpness, and their ability to perform their grooming tasks, are vital aspects to consider. However, several other elements need to be taken into consideration.

One of these elements for a dog groomer to consider is whether the scissor has been ergonomically designed.

What do ergonomics and ergonomically designed mean?

Ergonomics is the applied science of human factor engineering in product design. It maximises productivity by reducing operator physical effort, fatigue, and discomfort. A fantastic example of this in action is the computer mouse. This product is used (or used to be, as everything now is a touch screen or touchpad) just by using two fingers to click and move around in small areas with minimal effort. The operator does not even consider using it because there is no pressure from their hand or fingers. It is effortless.

So how does owning ergonomically designed grooming scissors benefit a dog groomer?

An ergonomically designed pair of scissors puts the least stress on the hand, arm, shoulder and back. The handles are designed to be **offset**, allowing the scissor to fit in the natural hand position, preventing the finger and thumb from moving and creating a comfortable grip. The spacing between the finger and thumb holes helps prevent the groomer's hand from cramping. A downwards bend in the thumb hole allows the groomer to straighten the wrist and drop the shoulder and elbow.

The Japanese stainless steels are naturally light, which is an extremely important aspect for the dog groomer to consider. In addition, it naturally removes the pressure off their fingers, wrist, elbow, and shoulder whilst using the scissor. This benefit helps prevent long-term physical damage to the dog groomer.

Chapter 3

~~~

TYPES OF GROOMING
SCISSORS AND THEIR USES

In the world of grooming scissors, many different types of scissors are available, and it can feel like a daunting task to decide which scissors to purchase.

It is highly recommended that every dog groomer has the four essential scissors: the straight scissor, the curved scissor, the blending scissor and the texturising scissor. This is to ensure that they have the scissors required to groom each coat type.

These four scissors will cover all dog grooming scissoring tasks on all dog coat types. There are many different variations of these essential scissors, and they are all designed to help create beautiful lines, shapes, and finishes.

It is important to note for scissors to perform effectively, they should only ever be used on dry and correctly prepared coats. This means that the coat should be mat or knot-free, thoroughly clean (so free from dirt, mud, grease and product build-up) and completely dry.

Straight Grooming Scissors

Whilst each dog groomer has their own preferences, straight scissors are fantastic at creating shape, and finishing off a groom, and are typically the best all-round or the most versatile of the dog grooming scissors family you can own. For pet owners who only wish to invest in one style of scissors, the choice should be the straight scissor.

Why is the straight grooming scissor the most versatile of the scissors?

A dog groomer can create a rounded line with a pair of straight scissors, which can be used on all areas of a dog's body. However, the blending scissor, chunkers and texturising scissors cannot create a crisp straight line as they have more specific purposes.

Detailing Scissors

Detailing scissors are the smallest of straight dog grooming scissors. These are small straight scissors, with lengths ranging from 4" to 6" in length.

These scissors are designed to be used for detailing work such as the dog's feet, ear edges, around the eyes and other areas that require tiny hairs to be removed.

Curved Grooming Scissors

Curved scissors are part of a dog groomer's scissor collection and these grooming scissors with curved blades can be a very useful grooming tool in preference to straight blade grooming scissors in certain situations.

Every dog groomer should have a pair of these ready to turn their doggy customer' grooms into wonderful works of art.

These curved scissors are designed to be precise tools that can trim in meticulous detail, trim a dog's coat smoothly and sharply without bending or snagging the hair strands.

What Are Curved Dog Grooming Scissors?

Curved scissors are excellent tools for adding angulation to areas of a dog, such as the head, ears, and feet and creating rounded shapes along the body. These scissors, like straight scissors, are suitable for most dog coat types.

These scissors are designed for working on fine details, rather than preparation grooming or 'rough trimming' a dog's coat. Due to this, it's common for these scissors to have offset handles, so the dog groomer can exercise more control while cutting.

Because the blades bend similar to the beak of a bird, they conform better to the curves of the dog's head and body, cutting exactly what is needed.

The 'bend', however, can vary and is measured as a degree of curvature or angle. A large number of curved scissors have between a 15 to 25 degree curve, which lends them to being an excellent workhorse scissor and perfect for everyday use.

The ever increasing popular dog grooming style, Asian Fusion, has made for the super or extreme curved scissors. The degree of curvature is far more pronounced and sits between 30 and 40 degrees.

In addition to the arc shape of the curved scissors, they are generally made with blades with convex edges. Convex blades are used to avoid bending or snagging on hair strands, ensuring that the cut is precise and leaves a tidy finish. For more information on the types of cutting edges, see chapter 5.

When Should a Curved Scissor be used?

What are curved scissors used for, exactly? Let's tackle the key reasons.

When a dog groomer is creating a trim on a dog, inevitably they will come across areas which require very careful blade work.

The curved blade of a scissor can be a better tool for cutting when a dog groomer needs to be precise, and that's simply because of the shape of a dog's body parts.

The dog's anatomy has a natural, flowing contour to them, and curved dog grooming scissors are designed to follow this outline so that the dog doesn't have any rough or uneven edges like a polygon.

Curved scissors are excellent tools for adding definition to areas of a dog, such as the head, ears, feet and creating rounded shapes along the body. These scissors are suitable for most dog coat types.

The Benefits of Using Curved Grooming Scissors

It's good to note these functional and ergonomic advantages that curved scissors have compared to straight scissors.

The dog's individual coat strands are less prone from slipping off the blade and are more likely to be cut at the level wanted by the dog groomer.

It's more precise when cutting near the ears, around the head, feet and on areas of the dog's body where angulation is required.

Compared to straight scissors, curved scissors can help produce smoother edges that give off a more natural look to the dog. A dog groomer will pay attention to how the coat should complement, rather than detract from, the dog's head, face shape and body shape.

In summary, curved dog grooming scissors do play a vital role whilst grooming a dog and it is highly recommended that a dog groomer should have at least one pair of curved scissors in their grooming kit.

Blending Grooming Scissor

A Blending scissor is designed to be between 6.5" and 8" in length and has between 40 and 60 teeth. Each tooth of a blending scissor is finer in width (compared to a thinning scissor- see below) and is micro-serrated (see Chapter 5) which enables the teeth to 'grab' each strand of the coat and cut it accordingly.

This scissor is designed to be a finishing scissor rather than a workhorse style scissor used at the prep stage to rough trim a dog's coat. These are used for the following reasons.

Making seamless transitions between two or more coat lengths.

A perfect finishing scissor and helps to create a soft, blended look.

Trimming the feathers on medium-length, double-coated dogs, like Golden Retrievers and Pomeranians, to look more natural instead of blunt.

Softening the look along a dog's skirt line.

The additional feature of the micro serrated teeth is perfect for linty coat types such as Bedlington Terriers.

Blending scissors are available in both the straight design and the reversible curved design.

The Reversible Curved Blending Scissor

The Straight Blender

These scissors are suitable for groomers and pet owners at all experience levels, especially those who are training to become a dog groomer.

It is important however for a groomer or pet owner to understand the difference between a blender and a thinning scissor, as they perform different grooming tasks on a dog's coat. This is discussed in more detail below.

Thinning Scissors

Thinning scissors for dog grooming are used to remove bulk or 'thin' a heavy dog coat by removing some of the density of the hair. They are a workhorse scissor rather than a finishing scissor.

The thinning scissors have a distinctive design where they have a smaller number of teeth and a wider gap between each tooth compared to a blending scissor. This gives the dog groomer the ability to cut off less coat per snip than they would ordinarily with straight or curved scissors.

How to choose the right Thinning Scissor.

When considering whether to use a thinning scissor, remember that it is designed to lift, hold the hair and only remove **some** of the dog's coat.

Thinning dog grooming scissors can come in either the double teeth (both blades have teeth) or single teeth sided (one blade has teeth and one plain blade) versions and will have one of the three numbers of teeth, 40-46, 25-30 and 20-24. These dog grooming scissors are designed to 'thin' the coat as the teeth and space between each tooth is wider (compared to a blending scissor). The number of teeth correspond with the coat type, so fine, medium and coarse.

(i) 40-46 Teeth- Fine Coat Type.

A thinning scissor with 46 teeth will remove more of the dog's coat compared to the 30 teeth and 24 teeth thinning shears. This scissor is suitable for fine silky dog coats.

(ii) 25-30 Teeth – Medium Coat Type.

A thinning scissor with 30 teeth is perfect for beginners, as it helps prevent the student from removing too much of the dog's coat. This scissor is suitable for use on most dog coats and is the most widely used 'thinning scissor' by dog groomers.

(iii) 20-24 Teeth – Coarse Coat Type.

A thinning scissor with between 20 and 24 teeth is designed to be used on heavy, dense or curly dog coats and remove a larger amount of hair compared to the 30 and 46 Teeth thinning scissors.

The Double-Sided Thinning Scissor

This type of thinning scissor has been designed with teeth on both blades and is perfect for heavy duty thinning on very coarse or thick coats. As the teeth work hard on coarse or thick coats, there is a higher possibility of the teeth blunting quicker compared to a normal thinning scissor or blending scissor.

The double-sided thinning scissor is a workhorse type of scissor, and as such, it will leave a very natural look to the coat. For adding a softer and tidier finish to the coat, it is advised to use an alternative scissor such as a blending scissor.

The Piano Tooth Thinning Scissor or the "Fluffer"

There is, however, a new design of thinning scissor which is an incredible exception to the rule when it comes to the world of thinning scissors.

This uniquely designed thinning scissor is the new 'hybrid' grooming scissor which sits between a texturising scissor and a blending scissor. Each of the teeth is rectangular and resembles a piano key. The tooth itself is wider than a thinning or blending scissor tooth, but not as wide as a texturising scissor's tooth. The gap between each tooth is also much narrower compared to a blending scissor.

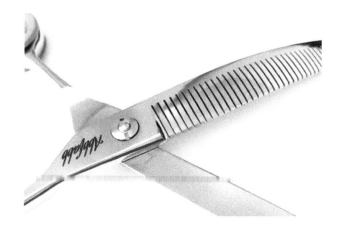

This scissor is designed to remove bulk quickly due to the broader teeth, like a texturising scissor, and helps creates a natural yet soft finish, like that of a blending scissor. It is a perfect dog grooming scissor for the new Poodle Mixed breeds such as Cockapoos and Labradoodles. It is also suitable to use on most dog coat types, making it very versatile and an amazing addition to a dog groomer's scissor collection.

Is there a difference between a thinning scissor and a blending scissor?

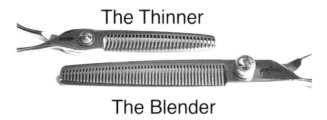

The Thinner

The Blender

Thinning scissors and blending scissors do look physically similar as they both share two of the different teeth designs and the micro-serrated cutting edge.

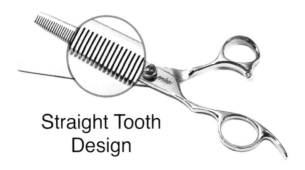

Straight Tooth Design

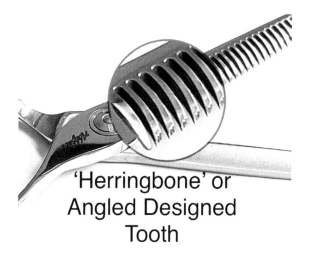

'Herringbone' or
Angled Designed
Tooth

However, these two types of scissors can cause a little confusion and their names are used incorrectly.

When choosing between these two types of scissors, it is advised that the groomer must consider the coat type they will be working on and the finish they are looking to achieve. A thinning scissor is a workhorse style of scissor and is used to 'thin' or 'remove bulk' from the coat. A blending scissor is a finishing scissor and is used to create a softer and smoother finish.

Texturising Grooming Scissors

Texturising scissors are designed to have less teeth, wider individual teeth and wider gaps between the teeth compared to a thinning or blending scissor.

The blades of this scissor can vary in length from 7" and 8" with between 20 to 35 wider teeth on the top blade. The tooth and the shape of the gap design of this scissor follows the coat's natural pattern on dogs with thick and wavy or curly coats.

As this scissor is designed for thicker and/or wavy coat types, they produce a textured and softer yet natural finish to a coat, which is a different appearance to the sharp tailored finish achieved with a straight or curved blade scissor.

This variety of scissor is available in both a Straight design and a Reversible Curved design.

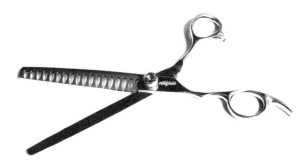

Straight Design

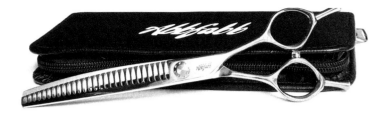

Reversible Curved Design.

The Chunker

This scissor is typically between 5" and 6.5" in length, with 6 and 18 teeth, with very wide teeth and very wide gap between each tooth.

These scissors are designed to create a very natural appearance. For example, a West Highland White or Cairn Terrier head, used with extreme caution, will add a chunky and very natural finish. It is advised that this scissor type is not one to be used by a groomer who is training to become a dog groomer. If this scissor is used incorrectly, it can remove too much coat and produce a very untidy finish. Like the Texturising scissor, the Chunker is available in the straight and reversible curved designs.

The Straight Chunker

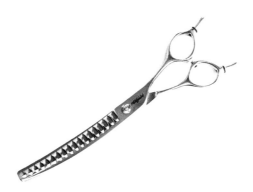

The Reversible Curved Chunker

Is there a difference between Chunkers and Texturising Scissors?

Simply yes, there is a difference between the Chunker and the Texturising Scissor. The names, however, used for these two different types of scissors are often confused and used incorrectly.

The Chunker

The Texturiser

Physically these two scissors look different, and they produce very different trims. They do, however, share some similarities in their tooth design and the fact that the cutting edge of each tooth is flat and not micro-serrated. This allows the scissors to give a more natural and softer appearance to a coat.

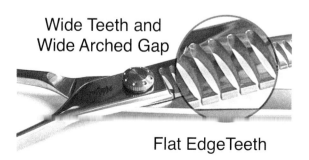

Wide Teeth and Wide Arched Gap

Flat EdgeTeeth

Reversible Scissors

What are reversible scissors?

The reversible scissors are a very popular style of grooming scissors. The reason for this is because they are uniquely designed to allow the dog groomer to use the scissor in ANY direction.

What does 'reversible' or 'flippable' mean?

Reversible scissors are engineered using two cutting edged blades with dual finger rests on both finger holes. In other words, the scissors are flippable and can be 'flipped'.

An example of the dual handles of reversible scissors.

Non-reversible scissors are designed with one finger rest.

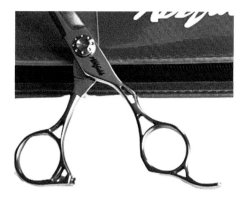

Both the reversible and non-reversible designs are available for right and left-handed dog groomers alike.

An example of a reversible scissor is the 7" Reversible Curved Fluffer.

Position 1 – Curve Facing Downwards.

Position 2 – Curve Facing Upwards/Reversed/Flipped.

How does a reversible scissor benefit a dog groomer?

Using a reversible grooming scissor helps eliminate the twisting of the arm into uncomfortable positions to get the blades moving in a particular direction. The reversible dog grooming scissors allow the dog groomer to influence the coat up or down depending on how the blades are directed.

The finger rests on both finger holes provide additional comfort and enable the dog groomer to cut in different directions with ease and help create a balanced finish.

Chapter 4

~~~

RIGHT AND LEFT-HANDED SCISSORS

Is there a difference?

This may seem silly, but there are fundamental differences between right- and left-handed scissors. As such, it is essential to ensure the dog groomer purchases the correct scissor orientation for their laterality. Most humans are right-handed, so most dog grooming scissors have been designed in the right-handed model.

However, for left-handed dog groomers, using right-handed scissors can harm the grooming quality and the calibre of the finishes, can cause damage to the scissors, and can cause unnecessary aches and pains to the dog groomer. This is because the cutting edges of the blades for a right-handed scissor are on the opposite side. As a result, the groomer will find that they have to apply a lot of pressure to get the blades to cut, which will blunt the edges very quickly and potentially damage the scissor.

Suppose the dog groomer uses the scissors upside-down to ensure the cutting edges are on the right side; this will mean that the groomer is not getting the full benefit of the scissor and, again, can cause issues for the scissor and the dog groomer.

It is advised that if a dog groomer is naturally left-handed, they should always use left-handed scissors. It will help them learn the art of dog grooming using the correct scissors, help build their confidence and help create wonderful grooms: happy dogs, happy customers, and happy groomers.

How to tell a Right-Handed Scissor from a Left-Handed Scissor.

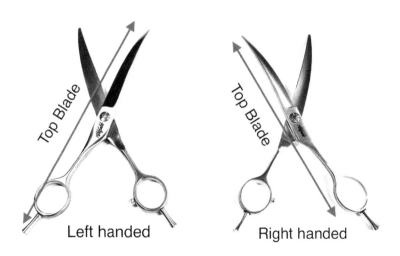

The difference is where cutting edges of the blades are placed.

So, to put it shortly, when compared to right-handed scissors, left-handed scissors have their blades 'switched'. On a right-handed scissor, the top blade has the handle type and the finger rest pointing towards the right, with the bottom blade housing the thumb hole. The cutting edges will be found on the inside of each blade.

On a left-handed scissor, the blade, handle type and finger rest are on the top blade but pointing to the left, with the bottom blade housing the thumb hole. A tip to help spot the difference is to note which hole the bumper rests on. It will always rest on the thumb hole and be part of the handle on the bottom blade.

Chapter 5

~~~~

DIFFERENT TYPES OF CUTTING EDGES ON A BLADE

With grooming scissors, there are three different types of cutting edges used in the scissors' designs.

The cutting edge of the blade is the sharp part and is located along the entire length of the inner of the blade (see chapter 1).

Convex Edge

A convex edge is slightly rounded (hence the name convex) as it tapers off to the finest point of the cutting edge along the blade. The convex edge is superior to other types due to its longer-lasting durability and the reduced drag when cutting. This type of edge is perfect for dog grooming scissors as it works on cutting through naturally coarse coats and performs beautifully with all scissoring techniques.

The only downside to a convex blade is that it can lose its edge if not handled or stored correctly. Also, applying too much pressure from the thumb, keeping the scissor loose or loose in the same pocket as other scissors, or dropping them will damage the blades. See below for more information.

Bevel Edge

A bevelled or German edge is the oldest and most long-lasting blade design. The cutting edge is very sharp, and the angle of the edge allows for outstanding durability. It is a fantastic scissor for blunt cutting but not for dog grooming scissoring; this edge does not maintain its sharpness for as long as the convex edge.

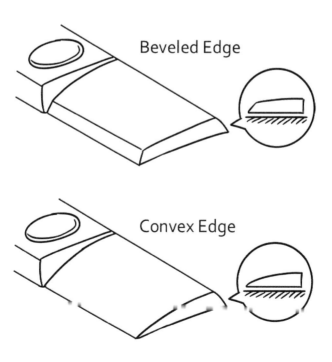

Micro-Serrated Edge

As the name suggests, a micro-serrated edge is a series of very fine grooves machined into the cutting edges of your dog grooming scissors, as seen in the picture below. The serrated edge has micro serrations along the entire length of the top blade.

It is advised that a dog groomer should own at least one pair of micro-serrated dog grooming scissors. It will not only contribute towards a sharp and crisp finish on the trim, but it will also give versatility in the art of dog grooming.

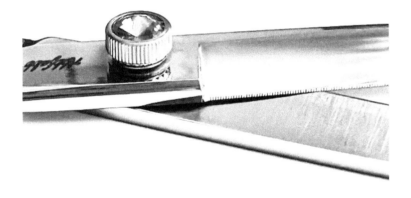

Chapter 6

~~~~

DIFFERENT TYPES OF BLADE TIPS

What is the tip or end of the blades?

The 'tip' is the point at the end of the blades, where they meet once the scissor has closed fully against its stopper (bumper).

There are three types of 'tips' to the end of a scissor designed for safety, gaining confidence, everyday dog grooming and creating show-stopping finishes.

Bull nose tip

As its name suggests, this tip type is rounded in shape. This design allows a groomer to develop confidence in using the scissors safely in close contact areas such as the eyes, ears, and feet. The only downside to this type of tip is that the wide rounded point does not allow the scissor to get close enough to create a crisp and tidy finish. Once a dog groomer has developed their confidence with the scissor, moving to a flattened tip or pinpoint tip will help take their grooming to the next level.

Flattened tip (Blunt end)

This style of tip or end of the scissor has been flattened or blunted. This feature is designed for safety, and despite the 'blunted' tip, the blade's cutting edge remains incredibly sharp. This end type is found on many scissor models, especially on scissors with teeth such as the thinners, blending scissors, texturising scissors, fluffers and Chunkers.

Pinpoint Tip

This style of tip/end of a scissor is the sharpest of the tips, and as its name suggests, the tip has been created into a 'pinpoint'. The design feature enables the groomer to use the blade's cutting edge AND the tip to produce crisp and tidy lines and finishes.

This design of tip is perfect for show and competition grooms. However, a dog groomer must use this type of tip with extreme caution, and it is not recommended for students.

How to keep the tips safe

To help prevent any potential damage to the scissor tips, the blades, the users, and the dog, it is important to ensure that whilst they are out in the salon, the scissors are close by but kept safe. Using a scissor holster or holder is one option, however, using a tip protector is another option to consider.

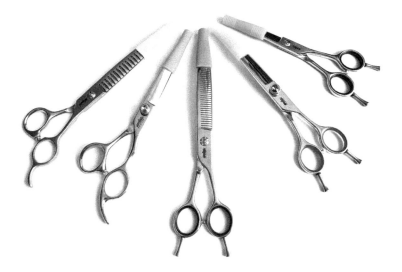

These tip protectors are made from strong, flexible rubber and are designed to house all kinds of grooming scissors while keeping the tips safe and the blades securely closed.

For overnight storage, once the scissors are clean and dry, make sure the blades are fully closed, carefully place the scissors in a protective case and keep them in a safe space in the workplace.

Chapter 7

~~~

DIFFERENT TYPES OF HANDLES

In the world of dog grooming, there are four main types of handle design. There is no right or wrong design preference as it just comes down to the dog groomer's personal taste and what they find comfortable holding and using.

When the dog groomer is choosing a pair of grooming scissors, they must always consider them an extension of their hand and how they will fit it. The shape of the handles and finger holes can help make a difference to the groom and the groomer's overall personal comfort.

The Classic (Opposing) Handle

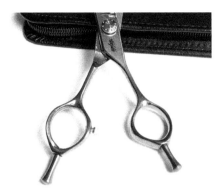

The classic (opposing) handle design is for groomers who hold their scissors generally with their thumb and middle finger. This handle design has been the only design available for many years. It has remained the most popular despite the research suggesting the possibility of hand and wrist health issues, such as Carpal Tunnel and other similar symptoms.

The Offset Handle

This handle design allows for a more natural hand position and is more comfortable to hold and use. It is preferred by dog groomers who mainly use their thumb and ring finger, me being one.

This handle design allows the dog groomer to use the scissor with a more relaxed hand position and has a shorter thumb handle; this automatically reduces the over-extension of the thumb and relieves any unnecessary pressure used to keep a good grip on the scissor.

The Crane (very offset) Handle

This design is angled to help drop the position of the elbow, which, in turn, allows for a better body position whilst using the scissor. Despite the lowered position of the elbow, the angled handle still allows the dog groomer to use the scissor at the correct blade angle.

This type of handle is an excellent choice for dog groomers prone to neck and shoulder pain. Continuous poor body positioning during a groom can result in several physical health issues in the short term and the long term. All dog groomers must take care of themselves.

The Swivel Handle

The swivel handle design is excellent as it does not matter which direction the blades are cutting; the groomer's thumb will always be in the correct position. In addition, this type of handle has a less restrictive feel and contrasts with the controlled feeling of the stationary thumb hole. Whilst this handle may help alleviate any aches or pains a dog groomer may experience during the day, working with dogs can cause unpredictable situations, so having complete control of sharp scissors is vital to the dog, the groomer, and the groomer's colleague's safety.

Chapter 8

~~~~~~

WHAT ARE FINGER HOLE AND FINGER RESTS?

The finger holes or finger ring is the location on the scissor where the dog groomer places their thumb and fingers whilst holding the scissor. For grooming scissors, the tip of the groomer's thumb sits in the 'thumb hole', and the fourth finger sits in the finger hole or ring.

The width of the finger holes can vary depending on each scissor's brand and model. If a dog groomer finds that their thumb and fingers move through the holes, using a rubber finger insert(s) or a Thumbthing or Ringthing can help maintain the correct grip and finger position during usage. See Chapter 11.

What are Finger Rests?

The finger rest or tang is the resting place for the pinky finger (small and fifth finger). These tangs can be either fixed (integrated into finger hole) or removable (can be manually removed if desired). These tend to be designed to be manually screwed in and out.

The Fixed Finger Rest

The Removable Finger Rest

It is advised that a dog groomer should check that the removable finger rests are tightly in place before using as they can become loose over time and fall out.

There is no right or wrong style of finger rest; it just comes down to the groomer's personal preference.

Chapter 9

~~~~~

WHAT ARE BUMPERS OR STOPPERS ON A GROOMING SCISSOR?

The bumper or stopper is an integral component of a scissor and is located on the inside of the thumb hole. The bumper is on all makes and models of scissors and on both right handed and left handed scissors.

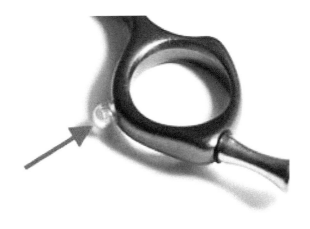

Why is the Bumper an important part of the scissor?

The bumper/stopper is designed to allow the grooming scissor to close fully and come to rest in the correct position.

The Correct Blade Closed Position

When the bumper is in situ, the blades will close fully without crossing over one another and the cutting edges will cut the dog's coat correctly.

What happens if the Bumper Has Fallen Out?

The Incorrect Blade Position

If the bumper falls out, the blades of the scissor will immediately cross over one another on closing and will fail to cut the dog's coat entirely. The crossing over will lead to damage of the cutting edges on the blades and negatively affect performance of the scissor.

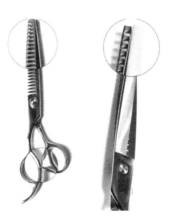

What should you do if the bumper has fallen out?

If the bumper does fall out and is not lost, it can be manually screwed back into place and tightened to ensure that it is securely in place.

If the bumper is lost after falling out, a dog groomer **MUST** not continue to use the scissors, as the blades will now cross over, will potentially cause damage to the blades and the scissor itself.

How can you help prevent the bumper from falling out?

The bumpers are liable to loosen over time and can fall out, so it is highly recommended that a dog groomer should always ensure the bumpers are tightly fixed in place before using, to help prevent them from falling out.

If the bumper cannot be located, a dog groomer should contact their scissor sharpener for a replacement or the company where the scissors were purchased from.

Chapter 10

~~~

HOW ARE GROOMING SCISSORS MEASURED?

Although the appearance and purpose of the dog grooming scissors are important things to consider when making a purchase, it is also very important to consider the scissor's length. In the world of dog grooming, the length of the blades really does matter.

Unless it is stated, knowing what size of scissors you should buy can be a little tricky.

In this chapter, we discuss everything you need to know about measuring scissors, how to measure scissor blade length and the scissor dimensions, so that it will be easier for you to decide which scissors will be perfect for you and your needs.

How are Dog Grooming Scissors measured?

Grooming scissors are made at various lengths to enable the dog groomer to use the correct length depending on the grooming task that they are about to carry out. To ensure that the groomer can purchase the correct scissor for the tasks, the scissor's length should be displayed either as part of the images or part of the scissor's description.

If however, this information is not available, the most precise way to measure a scissor is simply by using a 30cm ruler.

Place the scissor on a flat surface parallel with the ruler and make sure that the tip of the scissor is in line with the 0cm mark. Take the measurement from the tip of the scissor to the top of the finger hole, but do not include the finger rest.

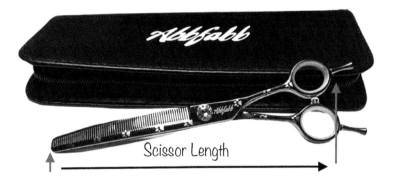

There is one exception to the method above: German dog grooming scissors are measured from the tip to the top of the finger rest.

Chapter 11

~~~~~

HOW TO HOLD
GROOMING SCISSORS

Why is the correct thumb and finger position in a grooming scissor important to a dog groomer?

To ensure that all scissors perform to their full potential, holding the scissor correctly is vital for a dog groomer to do.

Maintaining the correct finger positioning will result in the correct scissoring action of the scissor, and keep the scissors in excellent condition, helping the groomer feel comfortable and confident with scissors, helping maintain the correct tension, and preventing premature blunting and any potential damage whilst assisting the dog groomer in creating those beautiful trims and finishes.

The Thumb Positioning

It is important for a dog groomer not to place more than the tip of their thumb in the thumb hole. The reason for this is that the human hand is designed to 'grab' objects and hold them securely. Once the thumb is engaged with an item, it will naturally 'grab'. So, with regards to dog grooming scissors, this 'grabbing' action generates a large and unnecessary amount of pressure on the bottom blade, forcing it directly up against the top blade. This pressure will force the blades to grind against one another and will result in the blades catching or locking completely.

As the cutting edges of the scissors are extremely sharp, the small amount of pressure applied from the tip of the thumb is more than enough to enable the blades to glide smoothly across and efficiently cut the coat.

What is the Correct Thumb Positioning?

The correct thumb position is where only the tip of the groomer's thumb should be resting in the thumb hole. See the images below.

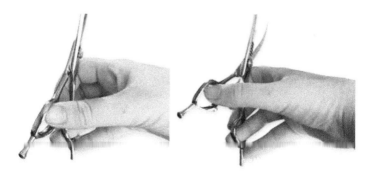

What does the incorrect thumb position look like?

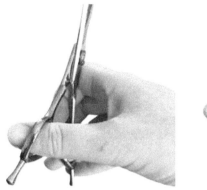
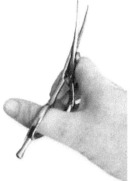

Technically, if any more than the tip of the thumb is resting in the thumb hole, this is the INCORRECT thumb position.

Using the incorrect position will cause the teeth to lock or catch up against the top blade and as a result, this will create a dent or dents along the cutting edge of the blade. These dents will prevent the blades from closing smoothly and effectively making the scissor unusable. To find out more about catching or locking scissors, please see Chapter 17.

If the dents occur and the blades will not close, it is advised that the dog groomer should contact a scissor sharpener and have the dents removed professionally. For more information on sharpening please see Chapter 16.

It is important to note that whilst using any grooming scissor, ONLY the user's thumb should be moving and operating the scissor. The fingers are there to help support and keep the scissor in the correct position.

Examples of Correct Thumb Positioning

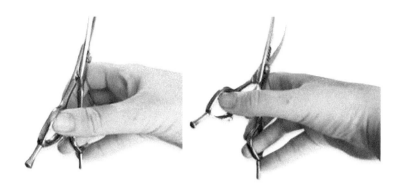

The Finger Positioning

The correct finger positioning is also an important role in the grooming scissor being used correctly and helps keep the thumb supported and in the correct place in the thumb hole.

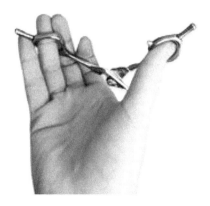

The Correct Finger Positioning

The Incorrect Finger Positioning.

For a free visual demonstration on how to hold a dog grooming scissor and the correct thumb and fingers placements, scan the QR Code below:

Scan for more info!

How to keep the thumb and fingers in the correct position.

As every dog groomer has different sized thumbs, fingers, and knuckles, maintaining the correct thumb and finger position in the finger holes can be difficult. However, the art of the correct finger positions can be mastered with regular practice either in or out of the grooming salon.

It is advised that those who are about to start to or are on a dog grooming training course, practise regularly (ideally away from the salon or training school), keeping their thumb and fingers in the correct places. This practice will help build muscle development in the thumb, as this is the digit which operates the blades, and muscle memory for the fingers.

It is also recommended for a groomer or pet owner to consider using finger aids to help keep both their thumb and fingers in the correct position.

What are Finger Aids?

As the dog grooming industry is popular for both men and women, some grooming scissors are designed with thumb and finger hole with wider circumferences. This is to take into account the difference in size of thumbs and fingers. This can make it a little difficult for a dog groomers with smaller fingers and thumbs to keep their fingers in the correct place.

There are a number of usual aids designed to help a dog groomer keep their fingers and thumb in the correct position.

Finger Inserts

The finger inserts are the traditional aids used by many groomers to help keep their thumb and/or fingers in the correct place and to help using the scissors more comfortable.

These inserts are made from either plastic or soft rubber and have been designed to be easily moulded into the thumb and finger holes of all scissors, enabling the dog groomer's thumb and finger to fit securely and more comfortably into the scissor.

Ringthings

The Ringthing is a brand new and unique style of finger insert which has been designed to be thicker compared to the standard finger inserts, to offer the dog groomer complete control and comfort whilst using their scissors. The Ringthing is a perfect grooming tool for reversible scissors or flips. The cushioned and rubberised texture of this Ringthing offers a dog groomer extreme comfort, help prevent painful friction between the fingers and the finger holes of the scissor and helps maintain the correct thumb and finger position and grip whilst holding the scissor.

Thumbthings

The Thumbthing is also a brand new and unique design of inserts which has been created easily fit the thumb hole of the scissor. This insert has been designed with a back panel which helps to physically prevent the groomer's thumb sliding through the thumb hole.

This grooming tool fits securely in the thumb hole and offers a dog groomer the ultimate precision and control over their scissors.

Chapter 12

~~~

SCISSOR SAFETY

As grooming scissors are incredibly sharp, there is a high risk of injury to the dog groomer, the dog or the surrounding colleagues in they are being used in a salon. Therefore, the scissors must be handled with extreme care and caution.

It is recommended that a dog groomer follow the seven Scissor Safety tips below to ensure the safety of themselves, the dogs, customers and their colleagues.

Eight Helpful Tips for Scissor Safety.

1. Use the scissors correctly. Remember they are not toys.
2. Correctly hold the scissors.
3. Practise finger positioning to help gain confidence in holding and using the scissors.
4. Where possible, cut in a direction away from your body, fingers, hands, arms, and legs.

5. If you need to share your scissors, pass them safely. Never throw your scissors! It is advised though you should not share any of your scissors.

6. Never attempt to catch a pair of scissors if they fall from the table, are dropped, or are knocked out of your hand. As heart breaking as this is, let the scissors fall to the floor, away from your feet and then pick them up.

7. Never pick the scissors up with the blades open, as the blades pose a high risk of laceration.

8. Always store the scissors with the blades fully closed together in either a protective case or with tip protectors.

Chapter 13

~~~

SCISSOR TENSION

What is tension?

Tension is the force along the length of a medium, especially energy that is carried by a flexible medium. Tension is an action-reaction pair of forces at each end of the said elements.

All dog grooming scissors have a tension system as part of their anatomy. Its purpose is to allow the blades to open and close, enabling the cutting edges of the blades to cut with ease. Therefore, all dog grooming scissors have a tension system, which plays a crucial role in the blade's ability to cut a dog's coat.

What is Scissor Tension?

Scissor tension is the 'force' between the screw that holds the two scissor blades together. It can be described as the looseness or tightness of the scissor.

The Tension System of a Grooming Scissor.

The tension system in each scissor is made of several components:

1. Stainless Steel Barrel
2. White Washer
3. Silver Washer
4. Copper Washer
5. Tension adjuster.

The Types of Tension Adjusters

All dog grooming scissors are designed with one of the two types of tension systems, a Raised Tension Screw or a Flat Tension Screw. Both types essentially help to adjust the tension as and when it is needed.

The Raised Adjuster

This system generally consists of five components: the barrel, a white washer, a silver washer, a copper washer, and the jewelled screw top. The screw of this system rests on top of the blade and is easily accessible to adjust when necessary. Whilst this system is very popular, having the screw raised can cause potential issues such as 'snagging the coat' or losing the tension if knocked by a dog or it falls off the grooming table.

How are the components positioned?

Step 1. The white washer is placed over the barrel and sits securely at the barrel's base.

Step 2. Align the two blades on top of one another with the barrel holes in both blades lined up together. To recognise the bottom blade, look for the blade with the bumper on the finger hole. The top blade will have the logo facing upwards.

Step 3. Feed the barrel fully through both blades and once in place, the tip of the barrel will protrude above the top blade.

Step 4. Place the silver washer onto the tip of the barrel. This washer is shaped like a bowl, and it must be facing downwards when in position.

Step 5. Place the copper washer on top of the silver washer. Ensure that the tiny notch on this washer is facing upwards.

Step 6. Ensuring that both the silver and copper washers are aligned with one another, gently screw the tension adjuster into the barrel itself. Do not force it into place. This will cause damage to the threads inside of the barrel and on the tension adjuster.

Step 7. Once the tension adjuster is inside the barrel, the notch of the copper washer will have fitted into the grooves underneath the adjuster.

Step 8. Using your fingers, carefully turn the adjuster clockwise to set the correct tension (see later in this chapter). As the adjuster is being turned, a clicking will be either heard and/or felt. This is a good indication that the tension system is now working correctly.

The Flat Adjuster

Like the Raised Tension System, this system consists of a barrel, a white washer, a copper washer, and a flat tension screw. The differences, however, are the length of the barrel and the tension screw itself. The screw sits within the top blade and enables the tension system to remain at the correct tension for a longer period.

How are the components positioned?

Step 1. The white washer is placed over the barrel and sits securely at the barrel's base.

Step 2. Align the two blades on top of one another with the barrel holes in both blades lined up together.

Step 3. Feed the barrel fully through both blades and once in place, the tip of the barrel will sit inside the hole of the top blade.

Step 4. Place the copper washer onto the tip of the barrel with the notch facing upwards.

Step 5. Place the tension adjuster onto the copper washer and barrel.

Step 6. Once in place and using a tension key, wound the adjuster clockwise to set the correct tension. Like the raised adjuster, you will hear and/or feel the clicking of the notch against the grooves indicating that the tension system is working correctly.

Incorrect tension. What does this mean?

If a groomer uses their scissors at the incorrect tension, it will feel either that the blades are difficult to close, or they feel very 'slack' and close too quickly.

If the tension is incorrect, this can cause various problems for the scissors and the dog groomer.

Premature blunting – This will occur and <u>sharpening</u> will be needed immediately.

Catching or locking. This can be a result of incorrect tension and the scissor's teeth or blades will be 'forced' against the opposing blade.

If the tension is too loose, this can result in the system falling apart and the components being lost or broken.

Why should you always check and adjust the tension?

If the scissor's tension is too tight or tense, the blades will become stiff and not move freely. This will result in unnecessary wearing down of the scissor and will cause fatigue for the dog groomer due to the extra effort required to move the blades. On the other hand, if the scissor is too loose, this will result in the blades closing too quickly and will cause the hair to fold rather than be cut.

How to CHECK the tension.

To check a scissor's tension, if right-handed, hold the scissor in the left hand and ensure that it is held with its handle and blades facing upwards. If checking a left-handed scissor, hold the scissor in the right hand.

Using the opposite hand, carefully open the top blade so that it is sitting at approximately 90 degrees.

Release the top blade and allow it to close freely. If the tension is correct, the blade will stop closing at approximately 45 degrees or two-thirds closed – see diagram 1 below.

Diagram 1. Correct Scissor Tension

How do the blades close if the scissor's tension is too loose?

If a dog grooming scissor's tension is too loose, once the top blade has been released, it will not close, almost 'slam' against the bottom blade.

In diagram 2 it demonstrates what the scissor will look like if the tension is too loose.

Diagram 2. Tension is Too Loose

How do the blades close if the scissor's tension is too tight?

If a dog grooming scissor's tension is too tight, once the top blade has been released, it will not move freely and will appear to remain wide open rather than closing towards the bottom blade (see diagram 3).

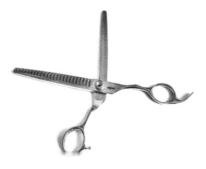

Diagram 3. Tension is Too Tight.

After a time, the scissor's tension will naturally begin to loosen so it is recommended that the dog groomer test their scissor's tension at the start of each working day and during the day after a long grooming session.

How to ADJUST the tension.

Most dog grooming scissor blades are designed with a slight curvature (convex edges). When placed together, a degree of 'spring force' keeps the cutting edges in contact throughout the cutting action. This is referred to as the 'set' of blades. If the scissors are too loose, this 'spring force' is effectively lost, and the cutting edges lose contact. This action results in coat folding or bending rather than cutting.

Once you have checked the tension, if it is **too loose**, adjust the tension screw to one or two notches or click to the **right.** Retest and adjust carefully until the correct tension is achieved. However, a dog groomer must be careful not to over-loosen the tension to where the components fall out.

If the tension is **too tight**, adjust the tension screw one or two clicks to the **left**, retest the blades and repeat if necessary.

A great rhythm to help remember which way to adjust the tension screw is "**Righty Tightly, Lefty Loosely**".

What happens if the tension system falls out?

If the tension is too loose and is not immediately adjusted, the tension system may fall out in part or entirely. If all or some of the tension system components fall out, a dog groomer must ensure that they have collected each piece and placed them back in the correct order if they are able to do so.

If the parts are not set back correctly, the tension and the blades can be damaged. If a groomer is unable to find one or parts of the tension system, it is highly recommended that they seek the advice of a trusted sharpener or contact the seller of their scissors. Spare scissor parts may be available from the seller directly.

Chapter 14

~~~

A SCISSOR'S BALANCE

A grooming scissor should feel well-balanced in the hand of a dog groomer. But what does 'well balanced' mean?

It means the weight of the handle and the weight of the blades of the scissor should be equal and neither should feel more heavier than the other. This applies to when the groomer is just holding the scissors and whilst the shears are in use.

Whilst cutting, a dog groomer should not feel that they have to work hard to keep the tip of the blade level with the area that they are working on. Nor should they feel that the handle is heavy and uncomfortable to hold in their hand.

Working with grooming shears which are unbalanced can negatively affect either the finish they produce and/or have a negative impact on the dog groomer's own physical well-being, such as fatigue in the fingers, wrist and hand.

How to check the balance of a grooming scissor

The weight of the handle and the weight of the blades act as counterweights to one another, so whilst resting the scissor at the pivot (tension screw) on a flat surface, the scissor should remain still and not tip backwards or forwards.

This test is suitable for all straight scissors, curved scissors, thinners, blending scissors, chunkers and texturising scissors.

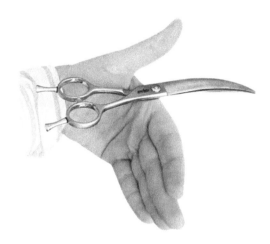

Is the scissor's tension and the scissor's balance the same thing?

Simply, no. A scissor's tension and a scissor's balance refer to two different aspects of a dog grooming scissor's anatomy.

A dog grooming scissor's tension refers to the 'force' applied by the pivot to ensure that the blades of the scissor glide smoothly past one another in order for the cutting edges to cut the fur. The tension can be adjusted manually by the dog groomer and is a vital aspect of the scissor's performance and longevity.

A grooming shear's balance refers to the weight of its handle compared to the weight of its blades. A correctly balanced scissor will have equal-weighing blades and handles to ensure that the groomer can hold it correctly and have the cutting edges of the blades cut the fur accordingly.

Chapter 15

~~~~

SCISSOR CARE AND MAINTENANCE

A dog groomer must always ensure that their scissors are cleaned at the end of each working day and placed back securely in a protective case for the night.

Cleaning your Scissors.

Using a soft, clean, dry cloth, thoroughly wipe your scissors after every groom. This will reduce the build-up of hair and products used on the coat, which may affect the performance of your scissors.

Use a soft damp cloth for end-of-day cleaning and remove all hair and debris from the blades. Pay close attention to the area around the tension system and where the blades close. A build-up of dog hair is very likely in this area. If not removed, the hair can rest within the tension system and potentially cause problems, such as preventing the screw from rotating when adjusting the scissor's tension.

Can a chemical cleaner be used?

It is possible to use a chemical-based solution to clean and disinfect your scissors; however, chemicals can harm the metal of the scissors and cause rusting and pitting. Plus, some substances are not eco-friendly. A handheld steamer or UV light is kinder to the scissors and will disinfect them effectively.

Once clean and before closing and storing, ensure that every part of your scissors is completely dry. Any moisture remaining on the scissor can cause possible damage to the tension screw system and increases the risk of rusting or pitting.

Oiling Your Scissors.

After cleaning and ensuring your scissors are dry, it is recommended that the scissors are lubricated or oiled. Oiling your scissors assists the cleaning process by pushing any remaining dirt, debris and hair from under the pivot (tension screws). In addition, it leaves a small layer of protection within the tension system.

Why should your scissors be oiled?

As well as cleaning scissors and ensuring the tension is correctly set, it is vital for a dog groomer to keep dog grooming scissors oiled at all times.

Keeping grooming shears oiled helps protect the metal from the number one killer of scissors... rusting, it helps prevent bacteria, chemicals and moisture from the salon from building up on the blades and in the tension system. The debris from dog grooming can also work its way into the pivot section of the blade, reducing blade mobility and causing unnecessary friction. Oiling grooming scissors can also ensure that the scissor›s blades are kept lubricated.

What happens if grooming scissors are not oiled?

If there is a lack of oiling, this will lead to the start of corrosion and rust will develop on the scissor. Keeping the scissors oiled will also prevent the blades from sticking. This will help the blades move more easily across the dog's coat and can help avoid snagging/pulling the fur.

How to oil your scissors

Whilst holding your scissors at a slight angle, carefully open your scissor's blades widely. Carefully apply one drop of scissor oil to the area closest to the tension system and allow the drop to move into the tension system. Once the oil has moved towards the pivot, open and close the blades to enable it to work into the system. Use a dry and soft cloth to wipe any excess oil along the blades. Ensure you do not have any physical contact with cutting edges for your safety.

How often should dog grooming scissors be oiled?

Oiling dog grooming scissors should happen each time the scissor has been cleaned and dried. Once the scissor is clean, place 1-2 drops of scissor oil into the joint section of the blade to flush any debris missed and protect the tension screw system.

What type of scissor oil should you use?

As all scissors are crafted from various types of more delicate stainless steel, it is important to use an oil designed specially to lubricate these stainless-steel grooming shears.

This is vitally important because many ordinary oils are made from petroleum and are made up of long and short chains of carbon and hydrogen atoms. As a result, under certain conditions, the short-chain molecules evaporate, and the unstable molecules oxidise and break down. Ordinary oils also contain substances such as sulphur, waxes and unstable hydrocarbons which can produce sticky residue deposits on the blades. This sticky residue can prevent the dog grooming scissors from cutting efficiently.

Oil made to lubricate grooming scissors is made specially using a process which alters the molecular structure to ensure that each molecule is uniform in size, shape, and weight. This ensures that the molecules do not break down and as a result, do not produce a smell or residue. This oil has been designed to produce the ultimate lubricant for scissors.

Is scissor oil different from clipper oil?

Despite what others may say, yes, the chemical makeup of clipper oil is very different to that of scissor oil. Clippers and the clipper blades are designed from more hard-wearing metals which move, vibrate, cut and heat up. As such the oil used to lubricate clippers is designed to help them cool down, keep them clean and disinfect them.

The oil used on grooming scissors is designed to be kinder and more lightweight compared to clipper oil, whilst offering protection from rusting and environmental build up on the blades.

These differences can result in damage to the cutting edges of the blades and not protect the scissor from rusting, bacteria and chemical build up if used on a dog grooming scissor.

It is recommended that your scissors are oiled daily to prolong the life of your scissors. However, always make sure that you do not use too much oil. Too much oil in the tension system can loosen the 'spring force' and prevent the screw from clicking when adjusting the scissor's tension.

How to store your scissors safely

Always ensure that the blades are dry and fully closed when the scissors are not used. This will help reduce the chance of accidental damage to the cutting edges and the risk of injury to the dog, dog groomer, or colleagues. It is important to remember, the safety of the dog is paramount.

At the end of the working day, after cleaning, drying, and oiling, fully close the scissor's blades, place them into a protective case or use tip protectors and store them away in a cool and dry area. Keeping the scissors away from the salon environment once the working day is over will help protect them from moisture, dust, hair, and debris which will settle once the salon is closed.

Chapter 16

~~~~~~

SHARPENING YOUR GROOMING SCISSORS

If serviced correctly and on time, grooming scissors will have a long-lasting sharp edge. Keeping them sharp is an essential part of any dog groomer's business. Dull scissors, when used, can cause untidy trims and fatigue, making it harder to get the best results when cutting every time. Sharpening the scissors will make a big difference in their performance.

When do your scissors need sharpening?

When your scissors are ready to be sharpened, there will be signs. If, after checking that the scissor tension is correct, any of the following problems listed below start to occur, this will indicate that your scissors need a little love:

- Pulling the coat or the coat snags on the scissor.
- The coat bends rather than cuts.
- They don't cut at all.

- They do not feel balanced.
- The dog groomer's hands feel unusually tired and sore.

How often do scissors need sharpening?

It is recommended that scissors should be routinely sharpened between every five to six months. The frequency may vary, however, depending on how often the individual scissor is being used. For example, suppose they use a particular pair of scissors on every dog daily. In that case, a dog groomer must visit the sharpener more frequently than for a scissor that is used less often.

However, it is recommended that a dog groomer should have their scissors checked immediately if they notice any blade damage within these months.

How to help keep your scissors sharper for longer.

Due to the very job these tools are used for, scissors will inevitably dull with regular use. However, it is possible to prolong the length between sharpening appointments by following these steps:

- First, always check that the scissor's tension is correct.
- Second, always use the correct thumb position.

- Third, always use the entire length of the cutting edge of the blade rather than one area. This area tends to be the top 1" of the blade.
- Fourth, keep the scissors cleaned daily.
- Fifth, oil the pivots (tension screw) regularly.
- Sixth, store the scissors away securely and safely.

Beware of over sharpening your Scissors

If the scissors need to be sharpened more often than advised (see above), there is the danger of the ride line (the area along the cutting edge which is sharpened) being worn away to a point where the blades can no longer be sharpened. Following the advice on how to keep the scissors sharper for longer will prolong the life of the scissors, reduce the number of unnecessary sharpening sessions and save you money.

Who should sharpen grooming scissors?

It is advised that a dog groomer must refrain from attempting to sharpen their scissors at home or allowing anyone who is not an experienced scissor sharpener to sharpen the scissors.

Sharpening grooming scissors requires specialised equipment, tools, and expert knowledge from a professional sharpener. Using an inexperienced person could cause damage to the scissors and cost more money to repair or replace them.

When choosing a scissor sharpener, this is what to look for.

As discussed above, sharpening your scissors is a vital part of the scissor's maintenance. However, finding a sharpener you can trust can be a little more complicated.

When researching a trustworthy sharpener, it is recommended to consider the following:

- Level and length of experience sharping grooming scissors.
- Knowledge and understanding of the metals used and how to sharpen these different types of metals.
- Knowledge and understanding of the unique scissor design and their grooming tasks.
- If the dog groomer is a left-handed groomer with left-handed scissors, does the sharpener have the expertise to sharpen them? Sharpening left-handed scissors is very different to sharpening right-handed scissors.
- Previous Customer reviews and recommendations.
- Do they have respect for the scissor and their design?

Your grooming scissors are an expensive part of the job, so it is highly recommended to always ensure that the sharpener who is chosen, understands all grooming scissors, respects them and knows how to sharpen them according to their individual grooming tasks.

Chapter 17

~~~

POTENTIAL PROBLEMS WITH GROOMING SCISSORS AND HOW TO FIX THEM

Like with any tool, a dog groomer may experience issues with their scissors over time. Below is a list of a few problems which may arise with the scissors and how to help resolve or fix them.

Potential Design Faults

Below is a seven-point checklist which should be checked by a retailer prior to sending any scissor out to a customer to ensure that every part of the scissor is in perfect working order.

Seven-Point Checklist:

1. Tips
2. Blades
3. Tension System is working correctly
4. Handles

5. Finger rests are securely in place
6. Bumper/stopper is securely in place
7. Cutting action

Any grooming scissor can develop faults during its first few days of being used. Therefore, always contact the company you purchased the scissors from as soon as you can and discuss the fault. A good company should be happy to help resolve the matter for you.

These potential faults are:

Premature blunting

Premature blunting is often the result of the scissor's tension being incorrect, too much pressure applied by the user's thumb, incorrect finger positioning or the scissor used on a dirty coat.

To help keep your scissors sharper for longer, always make sure that:

Your scissors are at the correct tension – See Chapter 13.

Your thumb and fingers are positioned correctly – See Chapter 11.

Never apply too much pressure on the finger holes – Your scissors are incredibly sharp and do not need any unnecessary assistance with their cutting action.

Never use your clean finishing scissors on a dirty coat. Only use your workhorse scissors for the prep stage or for the rough trimming.The fur can house grit, mud, grass, seeds, grease, and goodness knows whatever else, which can cause damage to the cutting edge and blades.

Never use blunt scissors. Using dull scissors will force you to naturally apply more pressure to the handles to get the cutting edges to cut. It is advised to have your scissors sharpened at regular intervals. For more information, see chapter 16.

Noise

The noise a scissor makes is generally not something to be concerned about. However, it can be confusing with newer dog groomers. Please do not worry.

Why do scissors make a noise?

All scissors make noise as the two blades glide across one another, as the action of the two metal blades passing each other creates the natural by-product of sound. The 'snipping' sound can vary in loudness depending on the types of blades. So, for example, the loudness of a straight scissor with two plain convex edges is naturally less compared to a scissor with one blade with teeth and the other simple straight blade. This is because the 'noise' from this action will naturally be louder as the individual teeth apply more pressure to the bottom blade as they pass one another.

The sound level naturally increases for a curved scissor with teeth. This is because as the angle of both blades passes one another, the pressure from the teeth onto the bottom blades increases. As a result, the 'noise' created is louder than two straight blades or two non-tooth curved scissors.

However, if the noise your scissors usually make suddenly becomes louder, this may indicate that they need to be sharpened.

Catching or Locking of the Scissor's Blades

What is locking or catching of the blades?

This is the action of one blade catching or locking against the opposite blade. It occurs more often in scissors with teeth (the blenders, fluffers, chunkers and texturisers). Still, it can also happen with straight or curved scissors.

Why Do Scissors Catch or Lock?

Incorrect thumb position. The thumb must **never** be allowed to protrude through the thumb hole as this will increase the amount of pressure naturally applied to the blade and pull it back towards the palm. This action increases the friction between the blades and will prevent them from gliding past one another. Where the friction is at its greatest, this force will cause the tooth, teeth or blade to catch or lock. See chapter 11.

Incorrect tension. If the tension is too tight or too loose, this will cause you to subconsciously apply more pressure whilst closing the blades. This amount of pressure will result in the blades 'clashing' and not gliding past as they should. Check your scissor's tension frequently and revisit chapter 13 for more information.

Blunt scissors. Using dull scissors will naturally force you to apply more pressure to the handles to make the scissor cut. However, this increased pressure will cause further blunting and could cause the blades to catch or lock. Therefore, it is advised to have your scissors sharpened every four-six months, depending on how frequently they are used, and if they start to feel blunt sooner, have them sharpened as soon as you can. For more information on signs of blunting, see chapter 16.

What happens when the blades catch or lock?

This action will cause the teeth to lock or catch up against the top blade and as a result, this will create a dent or dents along the cutting edge of the blade.

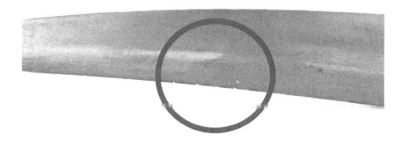

These dents will prevent the blades from closing smoothly and effectively, making the scissor unusable. If the dents occur and the blades will not close, it is advised that the dog groomer should contact a scissor sharpener and have the dents removed professionally.

It is important to note that whilst using any dog grooming scissor, only the thumb should be moving and operating the scissor. The fingers are there to help support and keep the scissors in the correct position.

The Finger rest/s fall out.

If your scissors have screw-in style finger rests (see chapter 8), the rest may become loose and fall out. After checking your scissor's tension, it is advised that the rests are tightly screwed in and manually tightened if necessary. If the finger rest does fall out and you cannot find it, replacement rests are available.

The Bumper falls out.

All scissors have a screw-in bumper or stopper on the thumb hole (see chapter 9) There is the possibility of the bumper becoming loose and falling out. It is advised that after checking your scissor's tension, check that the bumper is tightly screwed in and manually tighten it if necessary. If the bumper does fall out and you cannot find it, replacement bumpers are available.

The entire tension system has fallen out.

If the tension is too loose and is not immediately adjusted, the tension system can fall in part or entirely. If all or some tension system components have fallen out, ensure you have collected each piece and placed them back in the correct order. If they are not set back in correctly, this will negatively affect the tension and how the blades close.

If any parts of the tension system are missing, it is advised that you contact the company you purchased your scissors from or your sharpener for replacement parts and advice.

Parts of the tension system are damaged.

Like the rest of the scissor, it is possible for the components of the tension system to become worn over time or damaged. For example, if the notch on the copper washer is worn away, this will prevent the screw to grip and remain in place. Once this happens, the tension of the scissor will become very loose and will not be able to be tightened. It is advised that if any of the components are worn or damaged, do not continue to use the scissor and seek advice from a professional scissor sharpener immediately.